DECADES

The SIXTIES

Edward Grey

STECK-VAUGHN
L I B R A R Y
Austin, Texas

DECADES

The Fifties
The Sixties
The Seventies
The Eighties

Published in the United States in 1990
by Steck-Vaughn Co., Austin, Texas,
a subsidiary of National Education Corporation.

First published in 1989 by
Wayland (Publishers) Ltd

Edited by Roger Coote
Designed by Helen White

Series Consultant: Stuart Laing
Dean of Cultural and Community Studies
University of Sussex

Consultant, American Edition: Jack Nelson
Graduate School of Education
Rutgers University

Library of Congress Cataloging-in-Publication Data
Grey, Edward, 1949-
The sixties.

(Decades)
Includes bibliographical references.
Summary: Discusses the culture and historical events of the 1960s, covering
  the media, leisure, and such incidents as the moon landing and student riots.
1. United States—History—1961-1969—Juvenile literature.
2. United States—Popular culture—History 20th century—Juvenile literature.
3. History, Modern—1945- —Juvenile literature.
[1. United States—History—1961-1969.
2. History, Modern—1945- 3. Popular culture—History—20th century]
I. Title. II. Series.
F841.G67   1990   973.923   89-21618
ISBN 0-8114-4213-6

Typeset by Multifacit, Keyport, N.J.
Printed in Italy
Bound by Lake Book, Melrose Park, Illinois

1 2 3 4 5 6 7 8 9 0 Sa 94 93 92 91 90

Contents

Introduction   4

Fashion   6

Pop Music   12

The Media   18

New Freedoms   24

Youth Cultures   30

Designs for Living   36

Images of the Sixties   40

Glossary   46

Further Reading   47

Index   48

INTRODUCTION

The period between 1960 and 1969 was a time of teenage explosion. Young people were constantly in the news, whether through miniskirt fashions, pop groups such as the Beatles, tribal communes, rock music, or student demonstrations. Even the adult world began to change in response. People spoke of a youth revolution. And this revolution affected everything from music and clothes to sex, politics, and religion.

The events bewildered many people at the time. What was going on? Looking back it is clear that several different factors lay behind the changes. For one thing, there was simply a very large number of young people in the world. After World War II (1939-45), millions of ex-servicemen and their wives had decided to have families and this had created a "baby boom." By the early sixties those "baby boomers" had reached their teens.

Above *A long-haired youth demonstrates against the Vietnam war during a massive protest march in Washington D.C., November 1969.*

As their parents prospered in an expanding economy, teenagers found themselves with more money to spend. Clothing and music industries sprang up quickly to supply the young people's demands. Jobs weren't hard to find and teenagers generally did not feel the need to fight for their survival in society as earlier generations had done. They had more time and leisure to question their parents' values and to explore different ways of life.

Other factors also explain the youth culture of the sixties. Teenagers grew up with the real threat of a nuclear war as a backdrop to their lives. It seemed possible that the world might come to an end before they became adults. This had two results. One was the desire to enjoy life immediately rather than wait and put things off for an uncertain future. The other was to turn decisively against warfare as a solution to problems.

Above *An atomic test, photographed from above, at Bikini Atoll in the Pacific Ocean. Threat of nuclear war created anxiety, especially in the early sixties.*

Below *A teenage girl in the sixties. For many young women, miniskirts and long, loose hair symbolized new freedoms. Girls were permitted to treat their bodies with greater frankness than in earlier decades.*

In the early sixties civil rights marches and an idealistic quest for justice inspired many young people to become more active in a variety of social causes. Later, when the United States became heavily involved in the Vietnam War (1959-73) in Southeast Asia thousands of young Americans refused to join the service and go and fight. Some even fled to Canada.

There were demonstrations against the war throughout the Western world. Student riots were widespread. By 1968 it seemed as if the younger generation was in open revolt against the older generation.

So much has been written about the events that it is easy to lose sight of the larger picture. Millions of teenagers still respected their parents, went to school, studied for exams, and met their first girlfriend or boyfriend. Most of them probably hoped to find a place in society sooner or later, and very few "dropped out" completely. Nevertheless, attitudes and lifestyles did undergo a real transformation. The sixties were years of challenge and constant change.

FASHION

Around 1960 young people who wanted to dress fashionably usually bought adult-style clothes. Young men were still expected to wear clean, pressed trousers, a dress shirt, and frequently a jacket and tie. Young women dressed much like their mothers, in whatever the big fashion houses and department stores decided was in style. For casual clothing a range of jeans, T-shirts, loafers, and wind-breaker jackets were standard attire. Some schools had dress codes that did not permit the wearing of jeans.

Above *The ultra thin "Twiggy," a teenage fashion model, was one of "Swinging London's" most famous personalities.*

Boutiques, miniskirts, and casual dress

It was around 1963 that things started to happen on the fashion front. Increasing numbers of working teenagers had found themselves with money in their pockets and they were eager to spend it on records and clothes. While the big stores continued to emphasize traditional, adult-style clothing, a number of smaller shops sprang up. They specialized in ready-to-wear clothing for the new youth market, and were called ''boutiques'' (the French word for shops). In 1964, one boutique owner, London's Mary Quant, created the miniskirt. Meanwhile, in California, Rudi Gernreich introduced the topless bathing suit.

Clothes at this time were both imaginative and reasonably priced. Fashion trends changed very quickly and ''trendy'' became an ''in'' word. For young women the major development was the miniskirt. In 1960 hemlines had been well below the knee but by 1965 they had risen to several inches above it. The fashion shocked many older people. It also brought about another significant change in women's fashion: miniskirts left . so much leg showing that stockings became impractical, and Mary Quant introduced tights as a solution. Pantyhose also emerged to replace stockings and garterbelts. For footwear to go with the mini, the French designer André Courreges introduced short white ''go-go'' boots, which became quite popular at the time.

Miniskirts were usually worn with a skimpy top, and for the more adventurous, a see-through blouse. A jacket of bright plastic might be worn on top. In the mid-sixties the look was accompanied by heavy eye makeup, and perhaps false eyelashes. Hair might be teased or worn very long and straight. Some young women even ironed their hair to straighten it completely. The ideal was to look young and slim.

The miniskirt certainly allowed young women to treat their bodies with new freedom and frankness. This fit with changes in sexual freedom, something that some feminists advocated. But other feminists objected to miniskirts, as well as to the use of the term ''girl,'' because they considered such things sexist and degrading to women.

Below *Skirts got shorter and shorter, and were sometimes made of throwaway plastic material.*

The "Hip" look for men

Changes in young menswear were even more startling, because colorful men's clothes had been unobtainable before. The revolution began on London's Carnaby Street in England. While young men started to grow their hair, combing it forward like the Beatles, an abundance of dandyish clothes started to appear. By the mid-sixties there were fancy velvet jackets, striped hip-hugger pants, and shirts with long, pointy collars. Boots became fashionable. "Dutch-boy" caps were popular. In place of an ordinary shirt and tie, men often wore turtleneck sweaters, which were available in a wide range of colors.

The main trend, though, was toward a casual look. In the late sixties youth fashions had become so unrestricted that just about anything was acceptable. There were vogues for crushed velvet trousers, fringed vests, cossack capes, military jackets, Indian kaftans, and Mao jackets. Influenced by the hippies, some teenagers went around barefoot, and many young men grew their hair to shoulder length as a symbol of protest against adult society and authority.

Bell bottom trousers suddenly became popular at the end of the decade and the style caught on so fast that retailers could not keep up with the demand. Teenagers sometimes split their straight jeans up to the knee, and filled in the gap with a triangular patch of material. Colorful patches were also sewn in on the knees, seat, and sides of the jeans. Bell bottoms were often worn with a T-shirt that had been tie-dyed at home for psychedelic effect.

Below *Military jackets displayed in a boutique called "Gear on the Warpath." Anything with a Victorian or antique feel might be worn for fun, from long "granny dresses" to old-fashioned muttonchop sideburns.*

Above *"Dutch boy" caps worn by a young couple. The caps were made popular by folk singers such as Bob Dylan and Donovan. Notice also the psychedelic patterning of the woman's dress. The man has a decorative shirt and striped "hip-hugger" pants.*

Above *Rummaging for jeans at a boutique. The interior is typically casual, with garments arranged on open racks or heaped in piles. Older clothing and department stores were much more formal about displaying merchandise.*

The unisex look

One of the most important worldwide contributions to teenage style was an American tradition — denim jeans. By 1969 they were worn throughout the world. Levis were the prized brand of jeans. For the best effect, teenagers bought Levis that were too large and wore them in a tub of hot water so that the material shrank to fit. New jeans were bleached and washed over and over again to give them an old, worn look.

Jeans were classless; that is, they gave no clue to a person's background, whether rich or poor. And they were sexless, too. A long-haired boy in jeans and a T-shirt looked much like a long-haired girl in jeans and a T-shirt. In some cases, it was hard to differentiate between the sexes. But did that matter? By the time pants-suits for women appeared, people were al-

Above *Teenagers outside Kleptomania, a boutique on London's Carnaby Street. The store front, with purple paint and swirling lettering, was eyecatching in its day.*

ready speaking of a new unisex look with few differences between male and female styles.

Obviously not everyone wore the more extreme styles. But by the end of the decade lasting changes had occurred in the way people dressed. Boutiques had sprung up in most big cities, and even the department stores were selling clothing in the latest styles especially for the teenage market. Adult men might be seen wearing a turtleneck with colorful slacks; adult women wore their skirts above the knee. The youthful trends triumphed. At the beginning of the sixties teenagers had wanted to look like adults; by the end adults were trying to look like teenagers.

POP MUSIC

During the early sixties pop music was going through a quiet phase. For the most part the charts were dominated by recording artists who had made their names in the fifties, and much of the rebelliousness had gone out of rock'n'roll.

There was, however, one craze that hinted of things to come. In 1961, an American singer named Chubby Checker had an international hit with *Let's Twist Again*, a song that launched a worldwide dance fad. The Twist involved a lot of energetic hip-wriggling that offended some

Above *Chubby Checker shows how to do the Twist. The great center for twisting was the Peppermint Lounge, a club in New York City.*

adults. And it started a new form of teenage dance in which couples faced one another but did not touch. Other dance crazes followed — the Watusi, the Swim, the Jerk, the Frug — all with the same feature in common. There was no longer a need to have a partner if you wanted to dance.

Beatlemania

The performers who seemed to change everything were the Beatles from Liverpool, England. Their first hit, *Love Me Do*, only crept up the British charts to number 17 in 1962. But they had an exciting new sound, based on a line-up of drums and three guitars. The pulsing of the bass guitar gave it an especially powerful "beat" which began to catch on. The Beatles themselves were confident working-class youths with real song-writing talent and a lot of impudent humor. Their distinctive "mop-top" haircuts helped them stand out from other groups, and in 1963, with the release of *She Loves You*, they had a series of major hits. The press wrote of "Beatlemania."

Above *Twisting in the street. Many people believe that the craze caught on because it helped to release Cold War tensions in the early sixties. In this way it foreshadowed the "freak outs" of later years.*

Above *The Beatles, from left to right Paul McCartney, George Harrison, Ringo Starr, and John Lennon. In the early days of the "Fab Four" they performed in stylish, matching mod suits with distinctive round-neck collars.*

When the Beatles first toured the United States in 1964 they enjoyed the same wild success. This was amazing, because up until then America had always set the style in pop music. Other English guitar groups followed in the Beatles wake: the Rolling Stones, the Animals, the Kinks, and the Who to name just a few. Like the Beatles they had all been strongly influenced by such American performers as Little Richard, Bo Diddley, and Chuck Berry. The members of these "international" rock groups struck sexy, defiant attitudes that won over the hearts of young fans everywhere that they appeared. America as well as the rest of the Western world was conquered by the "British invasion" and young people flocked to rock concerts.

American sounds

Not all the big hits of the mid-sixties came from England, however. In California the Beach Boys had created a new exciting sound of their own, built around surf culture and hot rod cars. Other performers were starting to break onto the charts regularly on the Tamla Motown label. Founded in Detroit the Motown company rose to become the largest black-owned business in America with a wealth of hits by the Supremes, the Four Tops, Smokey Robinson and the Miracles, Marvin Gaye, Stevie Wonder, Gladys Knight and the Pips, and many others.

One of the most influential songwriters of the time was also an American, Bob Dylan. He

Above *The Temptations, one of many highly successful Motown groups. The company was founded by songwriter Berry Gordy Junior in 1962, and four years later was producing more hit singles than any other record label. Get Ready was among the Temptations' greatest hits.*

had made his name as a folk singer writing songs of protest against war and racial injustice. But in 1965 he started to perform with an electric back-up group instead of a simple acoustic guitar. His song-writing style changed, too, and he began to explore a moody, private world of dreams and visions. Dylan brought a new sense of poetry to pop, and his example encouraged the Beatles to write more experimentally.

Above *Bob Dylan was an enormously influential song-writer. Blowin' in the Wind was one of his early protest songs; The Times They Are a Changin' became a kind of anthem of the youth revolution.*

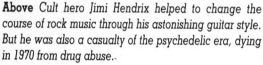

Above *Cult hero Jimi Hendrix helped to change the course of rock music through his astonishing guitar style. But he was also a casualty of the psychedelic era, dying in 1970 from drug abuse.*

Psychedelia

Bit by bit the most adventurous pop stars started to lose interest in the kind of music that was aimed at the singles charts. Recording artists concentrated more on albums, where they experimented with new ideas. The Beatles' *Rubber Soul* (1965) was a landmark, using the music of an Indian sitar on one track. Two years later the group released *Sergeant Pepper's Lonely Hearts Club Band*. This was an amazing creation, not only because it had a continuous theme running through it, but also in its use of a brass band, a symphony orchestra, and unusual sound effects. "Psychedelia" had arrived.

Psychedelic music sought to explore different ways of perceiving reality and to suggest dreamy and mystical states. The Beatles did not invent the idea. In San Francisco, groups such as Jefferson Airplane and the Grateful Dead were already closely associated with the hippy movement and were creating a new type of music. The Beach Boys produced a revolutionary album of their own in *Pet Sounds*. In Britain, one of the best-known psychedelic groups was Pink Floyd, which from 1966 on included a spectacular light show whenever they gave a live performance.

Guitarist Jimi Hendrix also created a huge impact through his psychedelic playing style. He grew his hair out in an "Afro" hairstyle, too, cultivating a look seldom seen on performers. New freedoms in music also brought female artists to the forefront including Joni Mitchell and Janis Joplin.

Musicians sometimes performed together at free outdoor concerts. Out of these grew the first giant rock festivals. Half a million people attended the now famous Woodstock rock festival held in August 1969 on a farm in upstate New York.

Above *Crowds at Woodstock, 1969. Rock festivals were a focus of the alternative society. Woodstock was held on a New York farm where half a million people gathered for three days of "peace, music, and love."*

Above *Pink Floyd was among the pioneers of psychedelic music. Long instrumental solos and weird electronic effects were part of the group's style.*

Back to bubblegum

In the sixties, rock stars were being treated in the media as the leaders of the younger generation. Fans themselves sometimes awaited a new album as if expecting new revelations about the meaning of life. Many fans looked toward these stars as idols. But the stars themselves were finding it hard to live up to the expectations they aroused in their young fans. The Beatles started to break up as a group in 1969, and in the same year Bob Dylan came out with a very straightforward album of Country and Western songs, *Nashville Skyline.*

Besides, the whole psychedelic experience had taken pop music a long way from most ordinary teenagers' concerns. After all, many young people still wanted simple love songs and dance music. "Normal" pop music could still be found on the charts. For example, Louis Armstrong had a big hit in 1968 with *What a Wonderful World.* But the psychedelic groups were the ones who tended to attract the most attention.

In reaction against the long-haired psychedelic groups, record companies started to bring out catchy singles again, aimed especially at younger teenagers. The Archies' *Sugar Sugar*, a hit in 1969, was a classic example of what came to be known as "bubblegum music."

THE MEDIA

Above *The Monkees were stars of a popular TV series. They were closely modeled after the Beatles.*

Teenage music entered everyday life through the inexpensive transistor radios that had first gone on sale during the 1950s. They were portable, which meant that radio was no longer something that the whole family listened to, grouped together around a large set in the living room. Teenagers could now listen to the radio alone in their bedrooms, on the beach, or in the street. In the United States, thousands of new local radio stations sprang up. Many played nothing but popular music, and some were even growing more specialized still. There were stations that played only Black music, or nothing but Country and Western, or Jazz.

Pirate radio

In Britain broadcasting was different from that of the U.S. In the early sixties, all broadcasting was controlled by the BBC (British Broadcasting Corporation) and very little pop music was played. To hear their favorite records, many teenagers tuned into a European radio station, Radio Luxembourg. This station did play pop music, but only in the evenings, and reception was poor. These difficulties, however, contributed to the special excitement of pop music. In the early sixties it was like a secret known only to the young.

Things changed in 1964 when an illegal, or "pirate" radio station was set up. Called Radio Caroline, it started broadcasting from a ship anchored off the British coast. Other pirate stations followed, all transmitting nonstop pop to millions of listeners. The pirates were banned by law in 1967 but by then pop music was so much a part of British life that the BBC had to establish a new channel catering to the audience. It was called Radio One, and many of the pirate disc jockeys joined it.

Below *A transistor radio on display at a big media exhibition of 1962. In the same year Telstar 1, the first television communications satellite, was launched and transmitted pictures across the Atlantic Ocean.*

Teenage viewers

During the sixties the first live television pictures were beamed across the Atlantic by satellite. It seemed that the electronics media were creating what Canadian writer, Marshall McLuhan, termed a "global village." Millions of teenagers, wherever they lived, might be listening to the same records, wearing the same fashions, doing the same dances. They might be watching the same TV programs, too, and television played a special part in spreading teenage culture.

For example, the Twist first caught on as a dance craze in the United States after it was seen on the mid-afternoon show *American Bandstand*. When the Beatles first arrived in the U.S. in February 1964 they were given extensive television coverage. TV cameras and photographers followed them as they flew into Kennedy Airport in New York where they were met by thousands of screaming fans. Disc jockeys played Beatles' music non-stop and gave updates on their progress through the city. And the climax of the event was their appearance the next night on TV's *Ed Sullivan Show*. It took them into just about every American home.

Favorite television shows at that time included *Doctor Kildare*, a series about hospital life starring Richard Chamberlain. Another popular program was *Star Trek*, a science fiction series featuring Leonard Nimoy. It ran from 1966 to 1969 and reflected the excitement people felt about space exploration.

Pop music shows were popular among young people. Dick Clark's *American Bandstand* featured rock'n'roll artists and teenagers dancing in the studio. In 1968 he introduced a new musical-variety show *Happening '68*. It was hosted by Paul Revere and Mark Lindsay of the group Paul Revere and the Raiders. Both shows were a showcase for performers.

Below *The Beatles on the* Ed Sullivan Show, *1964. Throughout the United States teenage males switched almost overnight from short hair to Beatle-style mop-tops.*

 Above Pop group Manfred Mann performing live on British TV's Ready Steady Go! This show was the British equivalent to popular American television shows, such as Dick Clark's American Bandstand.

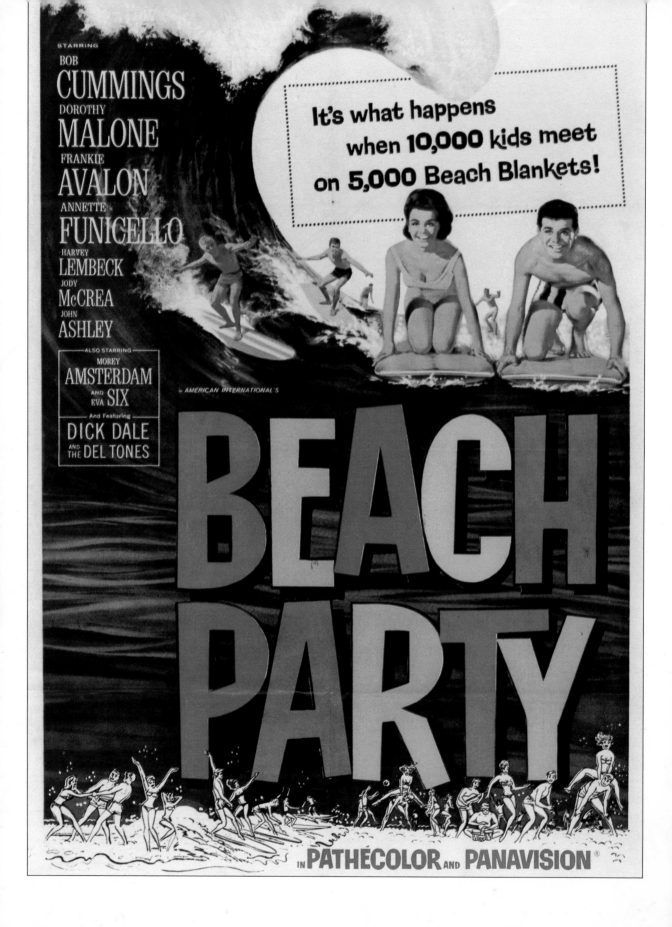

At the movies

As TV viewing increased throughout the sixties, movie audiences dropped dramatically. But films still had an influence on youth culture and reflected the changes that were taking place. In the United States, where many young people had access to a car, a host of cheap films were especially made for the teenage audiences who frequented the drive-ins. The "Beach" series was particularly successful. The films starred singers Frankie Avalon and Annette Funicello, and included *Beach Party* (1963), *Muscle Beach Party* (1965), and *Beach Blanket Bingo* (1965).

In Britain, American movie director Dick Lester made two very crazy, fast-moving comedies. *A Hard Day's Night* (1964) starred the Beatles, and *The Knack* (1965) was set in the "Swinging London" of the Carnaby Street era. The style proved so popular that it was imitated with the creation of the American TV series *The Monkees*. This in turn proved to be a great success and the Monkees went on to become international stars who appealed especially to younger teenagers.

During the sixties much more sex and violence was shown on screen than ever before. Older teenagers might go to see one of the James Bond films, which began with *Dr. No* (1962). Their mixture of action, humor, and expensive sets proved a winning combination with audiences. And the secret agent was a fitting hero at a time when many real-life spy cases were in the news.

Doctor Zhivago (1965) was a romantic epic set at the time of the Russian Revolution, and it started a fashion for Russian hats, capes, and boots. *Bonnie and Clyde* (1967), an adventure about two bankrobbing outlaws of the 1930s, made gangster-style clothing fashionable: Bonnie-style berets became popular with young women.

Facing page *A poster for Beach Party. The film was a big box office hit in 1963 and was the first in a series of popular "Beach" films.*

Below *Bonnie and Clyde set a fashion for gangster clothes. The film also depicted bloodshed and violence more graphically than many earlier films.*

Magazines

With so many colorful images flashing at viewers from screens, the printed word lost some of its impact and importance. The heroes of Batman and Marvel Comics were cult favorites among teenagers worldwide and Snoopy comic books were enormously popular, too. Toward the end of the sixties "alternative magazines" were produced for older teenagers, and often used psychedelic visual effects, such as colored type and dazzling backgrounds and included features about rock music.

There was a great vogue for satire, too. This form of humor ridiculed the stuffiness and prejudices of the older generation. *Mad* magazine attracted a big following of readers and poked fun at every kind of Establishment figure, whether they were politicians, members of the clergy or the armed forces, celebrities, or even average Americans.

NEW FREEDOMS

I n the early sixties young people might meet
at a dance, the movies, or a local soda foun-
tain. A craze for bowling spread from the United
States to Europe and bowling alleys also became places where teenagers gathered in the
evenings. Surfing was quite popular on
beaches in California, Hawaii, and Australia,
but it was hard to find ideal conditions for surfing elsewhere.

Above *Surfing in California.
The craze had its own slang:
a "hot dog" was a daredevil
and a "wipe-out" was a fall.*

Discotheques and love-ins

The first computer-dating agency made its appearance in the United States in 1965. The idea was to help lonely, single people find partners by recording details of their lives on computer files and bringing together those with interests in common. However, it was many years before this caught on.

One new craze that did sweep the world's cities, though, was for discotheques. The idea came from France where clubs started to emerge in which the dance music was supplied entirely by records played by disc jockeys, instead of live groups. Miniskirted "go-go" dancers often performed on platforms to set the mood. When psychedelia arrived, dance halls and discotheques started to use flickering strobe lights and other flashy lighting effects to create an atmosphere that complemented the amplified music.

But why go to dance halls or clubs? Why couldn't young people simply get together in a park or city square? The idea of holding "love-ins" spread from San Francisco in the summer of 1967. Long-haired young people would gather in informal groups with no specific plans and strum guitars, blow soap bubbles, or hand out flowers to passers-by as symbols of peace. Often couples demonstrated their affection for one another quite openly. Sometimes, the drug marijuana might be smoked, even though it was illegal.

Events and behavior of this type would have been unthinkable and certainly not tolerated in the fifties. Attitudes about behavior were changing rapidly.

Below *Dancing at a discotheque in 1965. Notice the Op art light show. Sometimes, dancers from the floor would get up on platforms to take the place of the professional go-go-dancers.*

The permissive society

People often speak about a new "permissiveness" that emerged in the sixties. In earlier generations, young people had been given fairly strict guidelines about how to behave in public, what was decent language, what books were fit to read, and so on. But now, those rules were relaxed. It seemed as though many standards had been radically changed.

In Britain a new age began in 1960 when Penguin Books decided to republish D. H. Lawrence's novel *Lady Chatterley's Lover* as a paperback. It dealt very frankly with sex, and an attempt was made to ban it. But in court, the jury decided that the book was not obscene. The teacher of a girl's school even testified that it was fit to be read to her pupils. The book went on sale, and after that sex was discussed much

Above *The cast of the musical Hair, photographed in 1968. The story concerned a young man drafted to fight in Vietnam who falls in with some hippies in New York's Central Park. Besides showing nudity onstage it dealt openly with drug-taking.*

more openly in books, newspapers, films, and television. Censorship of every sort was challenged. Nudity was even allowed on the stage when theater censorship was abolished in 1968. One of the most famous stage shows at the time was *Hair*. In this, "the American tribal love-rock musical," some of the actors appeared naked.

During the sixties the contraceptive pill also became available. It meant that women could choose to have sex before marriage, with no fear of unwanted pregnancy. Abortion was legalized in the United States and divorces became much easier to obtain. These changes seemed to encourage a carefree attitude toward sex and marriage.

New freedoms for women brought new challenges, too. The modern feminist movement dates back to about 1966 when the National Organization of Women (NOW) was founded in the United States to win full equality for women in society. A movement campaigning for homosexual rights also emerged at about the same time.

In the sixties outmoded distinctions between race and class began to be abolished. In the United States, civil rights activists pressed hard to obtain equal opportunities for blacks in education, employment, voting, and all aspects of daily life. Civil rights acts had been passed by Congress to ensure equality under the law, but it would take more than legislation to change attitudes. When James Meredith, a

black man, attempted to enroll at the University of Mississippi in 1962 he met with strong opposition from students, the University administration, and state government officials. Meredith entered the university on October 1.

Traditional religion also faced new challenges. Instead of going to church and accepting the authority of the priest or minister, many young people wanted direct religious experience for themselves. Some took up Eastern religions and the techniques of yoga and meditation. And there were other young people who experimented with a variety of hallucinogenic drugs—particularly LSD — to obtain mystical experiences.

Below *John Lennon of the Beatles, photographed in August 1967 with the Maharishi Mahesh Yogi. The Maharishi, a Hindu spiritual leader, founded a school of Transcendental Meditation that won disciples among young people. The Beatles were followers for a brief period.*

On the move

Young people often took to the streets to demonstrate, whether against nuclear weapons, racial injustice, or the Vietnam War. And demonstrations were not just ways of making political protests. They also brought young people together, and many friendships grew out of such events. People made their opinions known through bumper stickers, T-shirts, and lapel buttons with printed slogans, such as "Make Love, Not War" or "Black Power." The button fad began in 1967 in the United States and has never really died out.

Another new freedom lay in travel. Prosperity and advances in transportation meant that young people were able to travel around the

Below Anti-war marchers demonstrate in Washington, D.C. Mass protests brought together huge numbers. In America's biggest anti-war demonstration, November 15, 1969, some 250,000 marchers converged on the capital.

world more easily and inexpensively than ever before. Many young Americans went by plane to visit Europe. College students would spend summers in Europe, carrying all their belongings with them in backpacks. It was cheap to stay in youth hostels and travel by train or hitchhiking.

Hitchhiking was becoming increasingly popular. With new interstate highways in the United States, and motorways in Britain and Western Europe, it became possible for teenagers to travel long distances over land for free. There was even a dance fad called the Hitchhiker. By the end of the decade long-haired youngsters with backpacks were traveling to nearly all points of the globe, including remote and exotic spots like Afghanistan and India.

Above Hitchhikers in California. Increased travel by older teenagers and students helped to create the idea of an international youth culture. Long-haired youngsters in jeans with backpacks were a familiar sight.

The cost of permissiveness

The new freedoms created new problems, however, especially through drugs. For one thing, most drugs were illegal and brought users into conflict with police. Furthermore, many people who used the hallucinogenic drug LSD had "bad trips" — nightmarish experiences — or suffered accidents while hallucinating. Drug overdoses caused quite a number of deaths. Jimi Hendrix and Janis Joplin, and Brian Jones of the Rolling Stones were just a few of the rock stars who died, directly or indirectly, through their own personal misuse of drugs.

And in 1969 the press reported a horrendous series of murders committed by the members of a Californian hippy "family" led by Charles Manson. Clearly, drugs and free sex offered no instant solutions to the world's problems. A backlash against permissiveness set in.

Below A rally in London's Hyde Park, 1968, urging the government to legalize "pot" (marijuana). While it is thought to be a relatively mild drug, marijuana addiction leads to use of other stronger, dangerous drugs.

YOUTH CULTURES

Teenagers in the sixties did not all dress alike and think the same. Not unlike the way things are today, different trends led young people in different directions. Separate "youth cultures" arose, each with their own style of dress, favorite music, and type of behavior. They were almost like different tribes, and some were hostile to others.

Above *Long hair and face paints were hippy trademarks but by no means everyone adopted the style.*

Mods

The first mods emerged in Britain during the late fifties, and became prominent in the sixties. They were usually working teenagers, often with jobs in offices, stores, or banks, who spent their money on stylish clothes. They liked the cool "modernist" look of imported Italian and French suits. Suede shoes were popular, too. Mods had shortish but carefully cut hairstyles which were sometimes blow-dried or teased. The whole look was extremely neat, and true mods bought new clothes incessantly in order to keep ahead of trends. Their ideal was to look perfect all the time.

The boys set the style. Mod girls generally wore rather plain clothes, and a pale-faced look was essential. White lipstick and heavy eyeshadow were typical.

The mods made Carnaby Street in London famous, buying their clothes at a few stylish shops there in 1962-63. They drove Italian motor scooters — Vespas and Lambrettas — which they decorated with masses of extra lights, chrome mirrors, and fur trim. To protect their clothes they wore khaki parkas, which were warm and functional rather than stylish looking. Rhythm 'n' blues (R & B) was the mods' favorite music in the early days. American performers such as Muddy Waters and Howlin' Wolf were cult figures. Later, teenage mods formed rock groups of their own. The Who and the Small Faces are examples.

Mods sometimes took amphetamine pills which at the time were easy to obtain from doctors. Known as "speed" the drug tended to create a restless energy that often erupted in fights. Pent-up aggression was part of the mod experience. Pete Townsend of the Who often

Below Scooter-riding mods arrive at the English seashore town of Clacton in Essex, where teenage gangs rioted in 1964. The big, clumsy parkas were worn to protect the neater clothes underneath.

Below *A Hell's Angel. Gang members sometimes turned up to act as "police" at rock festivals, but things occasionally went very wrong. In 1969, at a free Rolling Stones concert at Altamont near San Francisco, a man was stabbed to death by Hell's Angels.*

smashed his guitar on stage in a fit of apparent rage that was probably just part of the show.

In the summer of 1964, masses of mods converged on the English seashore town of Clacton and fights broke out with smaller groups of leather-jacketed "rockers." Similar events occurred again in the years to come but by now the true era of the original mods was almost over. Before long, people were using the term "mod," especially here in the United States, to describe anyone who was young and fashionable.

Rockers, greasers, and Hell's Angels

In the United States lawless gangs of motorcyclists known as Hell's Angels evolved. Some wore Nazi helmets or war medals for shock effect. As the hippy lifestyle caught on in California, the Hell's Angels tended to grow their hair longer. Few of them were teenagers, but by the end of the sixties their style was being copied by small groups of motorcycle enthusiasts in other countries. The term "greasers" was sometimes used to describe them.

Rockers were Britain's leather-clad motorcycle riders modeled after Hell's Angels. Their style of greased hair, leather jacket and jeans went back to the fifties. It was the dress of both men and women. In fact, rockers tended to be older than the mods, and there were far fewer of them. Rock'n'roll was their music, and they made a point of not following new trends in music or in fashion.

Hippies

In the fifties, "Beatniks" had often worn sandals, scruffy clothes, and longish hair. The hippies emerged from this tradition. Jazz, folk music, and Eastern mysticism were all part of the movement, as were relaxed attitudes toward sex and drugs.

The first hippy communes emerged in San Francisco. They were made up of groups of young people who lived together, sharing their possessions and trying to create a communal lifestyle. It was to be based on cooperation, and offered an alternative to the competitive world outside. In 1967, beads and bells were worn around the neck and flowers were passed out as tokens of peace and love. In the rural areas around San Francisco, groups known as diggers emerged, trying to make a living by farming the land communally.

The idea of an alternative society did spread around the world, especially among older teenagers and students. However, few lived a genuine hippy lifestyle. And the Vietnam War made some want to do more than drop out of society; they wanted to change it through marches, demonstrations, and revolutionary politics. "Yippies" was a word coined to describe the Youth International Party — the political hippies who emerged in 1968.

Below *Hippies in love beads and ethnic fabrics relax in a San Francisco park. It was easier to live a leisurely "alternative" lifestyle in mid-summer than it was in winter.*

Black Panthers

The Black Panthers was a group of revolutionary young blacks, founded in October 1966, in the Bay Area of San Francisco. In other black urban sections of the country, angry blacks were willing to use violence in an attempt to change what they considered to be a racist system. The organization grew, and emerged at the forefront of radical politics, as a reaction against the earlier nonviolent approach of the black civil rights movement. The Black Panthers assumed a militant attitude in order to fight the establishment; many whites were fearful of this aggressive stance. Among a list of demands, the Panthers wanted better housing and job opportunities for blacks, and an end to reported police brutality.

Few black teenagers were members, but the movement did have an influence in encouraging young blacks to develop a sense of pride in their African origins. The Black Panthers' look, based on leather jacket and beret or Afro hairstyle, was copied even by those who might not share their aims. The Afro hairstyle was particularly symbolic. For years, stylish young blacks had been trying to straighten their hair to resemble whites. Now they felt free to be themselves and to look African.

Skinheads

In 1969 the British press started to report the presence of a new teenage cult. "Skinheads" shaved their heads almost to the scalp. They wore boots and suspenders to create a look that was deliberately hard and masculine, or even military. Sometimes skinhead gangs fought one another at soccer matches; sometimes they beat up long-haired students and hippies.

Skinheads were mostly working-class youths. They knew they could not expect to get a job if they wore long hair and looked sloppy. Like the mods before them they preferred a clean-cut look, but they took it to the extremes.

Psychedelia meant nothing to skinheads. Their views were often conservative. But originally they were not racist. During the 1970s, however, the skinhead cult became more associated with racist attitudes and with attacks on Pakistanis living in England in particular.

Left *The poster shows two members of the Black Panther movement wearing the uniform of berets and leather jackets. Panthers claimed that the United States government acted like a fascist (extreme right-wing) dictatorship toward blacks.*

Right *The skinhead look. The turned-up jeans and big Dr. Marten boots were key items of clothing. Music did not have quite the importance to skinheads that it did to other youth cults.*

DESIGNS FOR LIVING

The background to teenage life changed dramatically during the sixties. City skylines, for example, were transformed. All around the world, huge office buildings built of glass and steel loomed up over older buildings. The number of cars on the roads increased dramatically, causing traffic congestion in many cities and suburbs. Many new roads were built to ease this problem.

Housing changed, too. In many European cities, areas devastated by wartime bombing were cleared and slums were demolished. Families were rehoused in quickly constructed high-rise apartment buildings. After the sixties, doubts arose about the quality of life in the new apartment buildings. But at the time they seemed to be exciting developments and far superior to the old houses that they replaced.

Above *The interior of an apartment in fashionable Chelsea, London. Notice the white walls and coarse fiber floor covering.*

The modern look

Designers of the time favored a crisp, clean look in architecture. Key elements were light and space, and architects tended to avoid anything that suggested clutter or pointless decoration. The concept of "open plan" living caught on in homes and offices alike. The idea was to have as few walls or partitions as possible. Instead of wallpaper with busy, decorative patterns, white walls and ceilings were preferred. In the same way, new houses were built to include big plate glass windows instead of windows with many small panes.

Inside homes, designers utilized modern fabrics to create furniture and fixtures. There were coffee tables made of clear Lucite and colored plastic, and chairs had tubular steel frames and synthetic upholstery. Instead of paintings with ornamental frames, people hung giant posters on their walls. A poster was cheap and easily changeable, like so much else in modern mass society it was something that could be thrown away.

Below *The New York skyline. Skyscrapers had long been distinctive features of American cities. In the sixties, towering office buildings and high rise apartments sprang up to transform city skylines across the globe.*

Below *The bare brickwork, see-through table top and wire-frame chairs show design typical of the sixties "modern" look. Everything has been reduced to its simplest form to achieve a sense of light and space*

Artists often showed real enthusiasm for mass-produced products. Pop artists, for example, used images taken from comic strips or, as in Andy Warhol's famous picture of soup cans, multiple images of everyday objects. Op artists such as Bridget Riley experimented with abstract designs that created optical illusions. They were often done in black and white, or in bold, flat colors. The designs seemed to move right before the viewer's eyes.

Primary colors seemed to fascinate designers. The Union Jack (British flag), with its bright red, white and blue, was taken up as a kind of mod emblem during the Carnaby Street years. Pete Townsend of the Who wore a Union Jack jacket. This was partly a satirical gesture, for Britain was losing her world importance. As a growing number of new Commonwealth countries won independence during the early sixties from Britain, the imperial flag became a fashion accessory.

Alternatives

Not everyone liked the ultra modern look. Some people feared what was called the "technocracy" — the scientists, industrialists, and planners who seemed to be dominating every aspect of modern life. There was a great revival of interest in Art Nouveau, the design movement of the 1890s. This had used swirling imagery based on dream symbols, the natural curves of the human body, and plant life. Prints by the English illustrator, Aubrey Beardsley (1872-98) became particularly popular.

With the spread of hippy ideas, paisley patterns and Indian fabrics became fashionable. For a casual look, teenagers scattered cushions on their bedroom floors. Ordinary beds were disguised as much as possible; divans with fitted covers were thought more stylish. Some teenagers even dispensed with the bed frame and put the mattress on the floor.

Young people began poking around in second-hand and junk shops for inexpensive, unu-

Above *New York's Museum of Modern Art. The background picture is by Roy Lichtenstein, a Pop artist who often used comic strip techniques.*

Below *Colorful posters appeared in the sixties. Unlike old-fashioned framed pictures, posters were throwaway objects that could be replaced when they lost appeal.*

Above *A teenager's bedroom in the sixties. Notice the Indian bedspread. In the converted fireplace you can see a transistor radio and mono record player.*

sual items that might be used for decoration — as a means of self expression. For many older teenage girls, the ideal bedroom look was rather exotic with Indian print fabric used for bed and wall coverings, old-fashioned bentwood chairs, potted palms, vases filled with ostrich feathers, and beads replacing doors.

Younger teenagers did not attempt anything so sophisticated. A bedroom might include a transistor radio, fan magazines, and posters of favorite pop stars. If there was a record player it was usually a small, portable device with mono sound. Stereo equipment only came into widespread use toward the end of the decade.

In girls' rooms there was often one item that you would not see today: a gonk. Gonks were cuddly stuffed toys with big faces and no body, usually with a Beatle-like haircut. Teenage girls often made them themselves out of fabric and stuffing. There was such a craze for them in the mid-sixties that a film was made to cash in on the fad. It was called *Gonks Go Beat* (1965) and British pop singer Lulu was among the stars who appeared in it.

IMAGES OF THE SIXTIES

Man on the moon

On July 20, 1969, astronaut Neil Armstrong became the first man to set foot on the moon. He was closely followed by fellow American astronaut Edward ''Buzz'' Aldrin. Armstrong and Aldrin touched down on the moon in a special landing craft known as the Eagle. Meanwhile a third astronaut, Michael Collins, remained in charge of the main spacecraft, Columbia, orbiting the moon.

Back on earth an estimated 600 million TV viewers watched the event which ended a decade of tremendous advances in space exploration. The Soviet Union had put the first man in space. His name was Uri Gagarin and he made an orbit of the earth in 1961.

Above *The first men on the moon: Edward Aldrin and, reflected in his helmet, Neil Armstrong.*

Martin Luther King, Jr.

Civil rights workers struggled throughout the early sixties to win equality for blacks in the southern United States. Many states maintained a policy of "segregation." This involved keeping black and white races apart — in schools, housing, and buses, for example. Black people were also denied their voting rights. The leading organizer for civil rights was a black Baptist minister, Dr. Martin Luther King, Jr.. Despite being often beaten and imprisoned, King always pursued a policy of non-violence. His campaigns had real results and in 1964 he was awarded the Nobel Peace Prize. King was assassinated in 1968, however, and his death caused widespread rioting among blacks in cities throughout America.

The Berlin Wall

Throughout the sixties the United States and the Soviet Union dominated world politics. A "Cold War" was fought between them, with no battles but many angry exchanges of words. Since both sides possessed nuclear weapons, tensions often ran high. People feared the outbreak of a war that could destroy all life on the planet.

The divided city of Berlin, deep inside East Germany, was one crisis point. The city had

Above *In 1963, Martin Luther King, Jr. addressed 200,000 people at a civil rights demonstration in Washington, D.C.*

Below *The divided city of Berlin. On the left, surrounded by the Berlin Wall and barbed wire, are the sectors controlled by the French, British, and Americans. The Soviet sector is on the right.*

been divided in two following World War II. The Soviet authorities controlled East Berlin and in August 1961 built a concrete wall along the boundary with the western half of the city. Some East German refugees were shot trying to cross the Wall, and Soviet and U.S. tanks nearly clashed at a border post known as "Checkpoint Charlie." In October 1962, a separate crisis over Cuba almost triggered nuclear war. By the mid-sixties, however, the worst Cold War tensions had eased.

Paris, 1968

In 1968, student riots broke out in the United States, West Germany, Japan, Italy, Britain, and France. In Paris, the ''student revolution'' nearly brought down the government. The wave of unrest was started by overcrowding and other problems in the education system. But student revolutionaries went on to challenge the whole of French society. In May they took over the University of the Sorbonne in Paris, and gave their own classes in the lecture halls. When police tried to storm the building, the students set up barricades in the surrounding streets. Battles were fought, and there were strikes and workers' demonstrations. Weeks later, however, order had been restored.

Above *Students and police confront each other outside the University of the Sorbonne in Paris, 1968. Police reinforcements are waiting in the background.*

The Six Day War

The Middle East was also a troubled region. Since the state of Israel was set up in 1948, two wars had been fought between the young country and its Arab neighbors. In 1967, believing that another war was coming, the Israelis launched a devastating attack on Egypt. The Arab states of Jordan and Syria were drawn into the fighting, too.

The conflict lasted for six days in June, and Israel won dramatic victories. Vast new areas were occupied by its troops. But the war left lasting bitterness. In particular, some Palestinian refugees from the occupied territories turned to terrorist tactics to advance their cause. The conflict started then between Palestinians and Israelis still continues today.

Below *A Syrian tank and armored car stand abandoned near Metulla in Israel, close to the border with Lebanon, following the Six Day War, a short conflict with lasting results.*

China's Cultural Revolution

China underwent a great upheaval during the sixties. Under the leadership of Mao Tse-Tung the country broke with its Communist neighbor, the Soviet Union. Mao believed that the Russians had lost their revolutionary ideals and he wanted to make China a true Communist state, owned and run by its workers and peasants. He used youngsters known as Red Guards as his shock troops. They attacked government officials, university professors, and many other privileged people. Some officials were put to work as humble laborers in fields and factories. By 1968, however, disruption was so great that the army stepped in to restore order. Mao's Cultural Revolution came to an end and was replaced with more moderate reforms.

Above *Workers, peasants, children, and members of the armed forces salute Mao Tse-tung in this poster from the time of China's Cultural Revolution.*

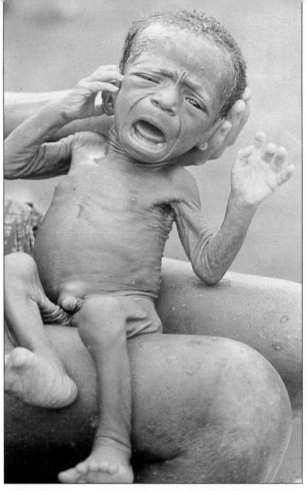

Above *An innocent victim of the Biafran War. In addition to those killed in the fighting, thousands of civilians died of starvation and disease.*

War in Biafra

A host of European colonies in Africa were granted independence during the 1960s. Among them was Nigeria, which gained independence from Britain in 1960. In 1966, however, massacres of the Ibo people took place in the country, and Nigeria's Eastern Region (which was chiefly Ibo) broke away from the rest of the nation. Under the leadership of Colonel Ojukwu the Eastern Region declared its own independence as the State of Biafra. War, famine, and disease followed. Many foreign nations lent aid to one side or the other; some sold weapons to both sides. The fighting ended in January 1970 when the Biafran government collapsed, and Nigeria was reunited. Estimates of casualties were over one million.

Death of a president

President John F. Kennedy was assassinated on November 22, 1963 while being driven through Dallas, Texas, in an open car. The event was particularly shocking because the glamorous young president was a symbol of hope for America's future. His New Frontier program of reform had promised civil rights for black Americans and more help for the needy. Kennedy also concluded a Nuclear Test Ban Treaty (1963) with the

Above *Jackie Kennedy bends over the body of her husband, President John F. Kennedy, after he was hit by an assassin's bullets. This picture is from an onlooker's film.*

Soviet Union, banning nuclear explosions above ground. Some of his acts have since been criticized. For example, he contributed to America's drift into the Vietnam War. Nevertheless, his assassination shook the whole world and many in the United States and abroad mourned his death.

The Vietnam War

Since 1954 the country of Vietnam had been divided between the Communist North and non-Communist South. Guerrillas from the North had been waging war on the South from the late 1950s. To halt the spread of Communism in the area, the United States government started to send in troops, and the numbers grew year by year. About 550,000 Americans were involved by 1969, and thousands of Australians fought, too. Massive bombing raids were launched against North Vietnamese cities, but despite the enormous effort the Americans did not defeat the guerrillas. Peace talks, which began in 1968, eventually led to U.S. withdrawal in 1973. The terrible sufferings of the war caused many people to doubt the government's policies and fostered revolt among young people both in the United States and in other countries throughout the world.

Above *A group of wounded American troops on Hill 875, Dak-To. The average age of American soldiers fighting in the Vietnam War was just 19 years.*

The first heart transplant

In 1967 a South African surgeon performed the first successful heart transplant operation. Dr. Christian Barnard took a heart from a 25-year-old victim of an automobile accident and placed it in the body of Louis Washkansky, a man suffering from heart disease. The operation, which took 6 hours, astonished the world. However, it was not entirely successful, for Washkansky died of pneumonia some weeks later. Though more heart transplants followed, it proved difficult to keep patients alive for any length of time.

Above *In August 1968 the Soviet Union invaded Czechoslovakia. Many people took to the streets in protest, including this boy waving the Czech national flag from the top of a Russian tank in Prague.*

The Russian invasion of Czechoslovakia

For many years the Soviet Union had exercised stern control over the countries of Eastern Europe. But in Czechoslovakia a movement for reform emerged when Alexander Dubcek came to power in January 1968. Dubcek wanted more freedom in the press, in business, and in the right for Czechs to travel abroad. His reforms worried the Soviet authorities, and in August 1968, Soviet tanks along with troops from other Warsaw Pact nations invaded the country. Although ordinary people demonstrated in the streets against the invaders, Dubcek's government was overthrown.

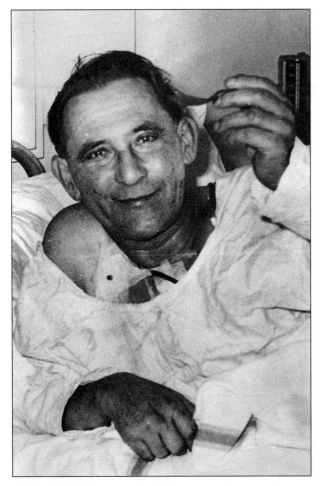

Above *Nine days after his heart transplant operation, Louis Washkansky smiles for the camera. Sadly, he died several weeks later.*

GLOSSARY

Abortion   An operation to remove a fetus from a mother's womb to terminate a pregnancy.

Alternative society   A different kind of society proposed by hippies and others in the sixties. It was to be founded on the principles of love, freedom, and complete equality of the races and sexes. It was also known as counterculture.

Baby boomer   Anyone born during the baby boom of the late forties, who became a teenager in the sixties.

Black Power   A movement begun among Black Americans to build up Black confidence and pursue Black interests through united action, rather than seeking help from whites. "Black is beautiful" was a slogan.

Boutique   French word for shop. The term was used in the sixties to describe the new clothing shops catering to youth fashions.

Civil rights   Rights that belong to everyone in a free society, such as the right to vote and the right to a fair trial. The aim of the civil rights movement was to win these rights for Black citizens.

Cold war   A state of fierce rivalry between nations, stopping short of full-scale war, especially between the United States and the Soviet bloc after World War II.

Commune   A small group of people living together and sharing their goods and possessions.

Communism   A political theory aimed at establishing a society where the major enterprises such as factories, mines, farms, and stores are owned by all citizens rather than a class of wealthy people. In practice, Communist societies have tended to create powerful state authorities to control those enterprises.

Conservative   A word to describe people who wish to hold onto established customs and values, and are cautious about any change.

Contraceptive   A device used to prevent an unwanted pregnancy. The condom, had long been available for men, but the contraceptive pill only became available to women in the sixties.

Drop out   To refuse to take part in ordinary society, for example by refusing to get a job or to finish school, or by avoiding military service.

The Establishment   A group of important people and institutions holding the power in society. Figures include big businessmen, politicians, church authorities, and military leaders. Overall, their views tend to be conservative.

Feminism   The movement aiming to win full rights and respect for women in society, and to celebrate the special qualities of the female sex.

Freak out   To become highly excited, for example, while dancing at a rock concert. Hippies believed that people should behave without inhibitions, even hysterically if they felt like it, and they did not mind being called "freaks."

Global village   A term used by Marshall McLuhan to describe the modern world, reduced to a single community by international communications systems.

Hippy   A member of a Californian commune. It was later used to describe anyone who dropped out, had long hair or wore casual clothes, and favored the ideas of the alternative society.

Homosexual   Someone sexually attracted to members of the same sex; particularly a man who is attracted to other men. Women attracted to women are more often called lesbians.

LSD   Lysergic acid diethylamide, a drug used in order to experience hallucinations.

Marijuana   A drug derived from the hemp plant. It was taken to experience a feeling of well-being known as a "high," which rarely included hallucinations.

Op art   Short for "optical" art, a form of abstract art based on techniques designed to deceive the eye.

Permissiveness   A view of life promoting the idea that people should be allowed to do as they please, with as little interference as possible.

Pirate radio   A radio station making broadcasts without authorization from the government.

Pop art   A form of art glorifying modern mass-produced images, such as comic-strip cartoons and soup-can labels.

Psychedelia   A distortion of the everyday perception of reality through hallucinations and mystical states.

Satire   A form of humor ridiculing prominent people, ideas, and institutions, especially the Establishment.

Segregation   The separation of people according to race, as practiced in the southern United States until the early sixties.

Technocracy   A system in which society is controlled by scientists and technical experts.

Unisex clothing   Clothes designed to be worn by people of either sex, whether male or female.

FURTHER READING

Rock Heritage: The Sixties, Chris Charlesworth (Proteus Publications, 1984)

Album of the Sixties Carol A. Emmens, (Franklin Watts, 1981)

The Sixties Reader, James Haskins and Kathleen Benson (Viking Kestrel, 1986)

The Sixties, Gerald Howard (WSP, 1982)

Dick Clark's First Twenty Five Years of Rock and Roll, Michael Olsen and Bruce Solomon, (Dell Books, 1981)

As Time Goes By: Living in the Sixties Derek Taylor (Pieran, 1984)

General background

America in Our Time: From World War II to Nixon. What Happened and Why (Random House, 1978)

The Glory and the Dream: A Narrative History of America 1932-1972, William Manchester (Little Brown, 1974)

Picture Acknowledgments

Barnaby's Picture Library cover, lower left, 5b, 11, 24, 25, 33, 37b; Camera Press cover, upper left, 6; Chapel Studios 38t; Kobal Collection 22, 23; Photri 5t, 9, 13t, 20; Popperfoto cover right, 4, 13b, 18, 26, 27, 31, 39, 40, 43t, 44t, 44b, 45b; Redferns 12, 14, 16t; Rex Features 7, 15, 16b, 32, 34, 42b; TOPHAM 8, 10, 17, 19, 21, 28t, 28b, 29, 30, 35, 36, 37t, 38b, 41t, 41b, 42t, 43b, 45t.

Index

Abortion 26
Aldrin, Ed 40
Armstrong, Louis 17
Armstrong, Neil 40
Australia 24, 44

Baby boom 4
Barnard, Dr. Christiaan 45
Beach Boys 14, 16
Beach Party 23
Beatlemania 13
Beatles 4, 8, 13, 14, 16, 17, 18,
   20, 23, 27
Berlin Wall 41
Berry, Chuck 13
Biafra 43
Black Panthers 34
Bonnie and Clyde 23
Boutiques 7, 8, 10, 11
Britain 5, 7, 16, 19, 20, 23, 26,
   28, 31, 32, 34, 43

Campaign for Nuclear Disarm-
   ament (CND) 5
Carnaby Street, London 8, 11,
   23, 31, 37
Censorship 26
Checker, Chubby 12
China 41
Civil rights movement 27, 34,
   41, 44
Clothes 4, 5, 6–11, 13, 23, 31, 35
Cold War 13, 43
Computer dating 25
Contraceptive pill 26
Cuba 41
Czechoslovakia 45

Dance halls 24, 25
Dancing 12–13, 20, 25
Demonstrations 4, 5, 28, 33, 42
Design 36–39
Discos 25
Doctor Kildare 20
Dr. No 23
Dr. Zhivago 23
Drive-in movies 23
Drugs 16, 25, 26, 27, 29, 31, 33
Dylan, Bob 9, 14, 15, 17

Ed Sullivan Show 20

Feminism 7, 27
Films 23
Furniture 37

Gagarin, Yuri 40
Gaye, Marvin 14
Gordy, Berry, Jr. 14
Grateful Dead 16

Hair 26
Hairstyles 7, 8, 13, 20, 31, 34
A Hard Day's Night 23
Hell's Angels 32
Hendrix, Jimi 16, 29
Hippies 4, 16, 26, 29, 30, 33,
   34, 38
Homosexuality 27
Howlin' Wolf 31

Jeans 6, 8, 10, 11
Jefferson Airplane 16
Jones, Brian 29
Joplin, Janis, 16, 29

Kennedy, John F. 44
King, Dr. Martin Luther, Jr. 41
Kinks 13

Lady Chatterley trial 26
Lichtenstein, Roy 38
Little Richard 13

McLuhan, Marshall 20
Magazines 23, 39
Maharishi Mahesh Yogi 27
Manson, Charles 29
Mao Tse-tung 43
Miniskirts 4, 5, 7, 25
Mitchell, Joni 16
Mods 21, 31-2
Monkees 18, 2 3
Moon landing 40
Muddy Waters 31

National Organization of
   Women (NOW) 27
Nuclear weapons 5, 28

Op art 25, 37

Paris riots 42
Permissiveness 26–27, 29
Pink Floyd 16, 17
Pirate radio 19
Pop art 37, 38
Pop music 4, 5, 12–17, 18, 19,
   20, 34
Posters 37, 38, 39
Psychedelia 16, 17, 25

Quant, Mary 7

Radio 18–19
Richard, Cliff 28
Riley, Bridget 37
Rockers 32
Rolling Stones 13, 29, 32

Sex 4, 26, 27, 33
Six Day War 42
Skinheads 34, 35
Small Faces 31
Soviet Union 41, 44, 45
Star Trek 20
Supremes 14
Surfing 14, 24

Tamia Motown 14
Television 18, 20, 21, 23
Temptations 14
Townsend, Pete 32, 37
Transistor radios 18, 19, 39
Twiggy 6
Twist 12–13, 20

Unisex style 11
United States 5, 6, 11, 13, 14,
   16, 18, 20, 23, 24, 25, 27, 28,
   32, 33, 34, 37, 40, 41, 42, 44

Vietnam War 4, 5, 26, 28, 33, 44

Warhol, Andy 37
Washkansky, Louis 45
Who 13, 31, 32, 37
Wonder, Stevie 14
Woodstock festival 16